MARRIAGE LINES

Notes of a Student Husband

ALDINE PAPERBACKS

OGDEN NASH

Marriage Lines

Notes of a Student Husband

J. M. DENT & SONS LTD

The following selections originally appeared in *The New Yorker*:

"They Won't Believe, on New Year's Eve, That New Year's Day Will Come What May"; "How Can Echo Answer What Echo Cannot Hear?"; "The Middle"; "How to Be Married Without a Spouse, *or* Mr. Kipling, What Have You Done with Mr. Hauksbee?"

Printed in Great Britain by Lowe & Brydone (Printers) Ltd, London, for J. M. DENT & SONS LTD, Aldine House, Bedford Street, London. This collection first published in Great Britain, 1964. Paperback edition 1968

SBN : 460 02077 3

FOREWORD

AFTER a third of a century of marriage I find myself still a student husband. I have done my reading, my research and my homework; I have tangled with trial and error, theory and practice. Experiment for experiment, I will match my record with that of Madame Curie or Dr. Salk. Yet today I feel as far from my diploma as on that afternoon in June when I stood at the altar in a state of mingled triumph and trepidation. As my own examiner I have given myself passing marks in a tidy number of tests, but I have had to flunk myself in too many others; there still remains an alarming host of subjects in which I have a vast amount of work to make up simply to stay in the class.

I have the best of reasons for wanting to be graduated, if not with honors, with at least a respectable degree. At a dinner dance in November of 1928 I surreptitiously shifted my place card at the table while my hostess's back was turned so that I might sit next to a girl I had met during cocktails. Fortunately she did not realize that I had substituted myself for her allotted companion, a rich and handsome former Princeton fullback, and I was able to attract her attention with well-phrased laudatory remarks about Al Smith and P. G. Wodehouse, remarks which changed imperceptibly into other and more personal compliments. My aim was then, as it is now, to persuade her to stay beside me for the rest of my life. In this I have so far succeeded, though there have been moments when she must have rebelled against being the major course selected for self-improvement by a perpetual undergraduate. Still here she is, here we are, and I have hope for the future, since I can now call up the fascination of the grandchildren to reinforce my own fading charms.

It has occurred to me that my notes jotted down through the years might help other student husbands. All of them have been printed before in publications available to the general as well as the scholarly reader, but they are here gathered together for the first time, presented in rough chronological order. Most of them are the result of long and earnest observation of the endearing but baffling feminine charm of one wife in particular and the equally baffling non-masculine peculiarities of many wives in general. I believe that the myopia and obtuseness of the observer increase rather than decrease the value of his notes. In the matter of wives, to know all is to be forgiven nothing. An occasionally lucky guess as to what makes a wife tick is the best a man can hope for, and even then, no sooner has he learned how to cope with the tick than she tocks. She is also likely to strike 11 at 6 o'clock and turn out to be right because she was thinking in terms of Paris time.

There are no conclusions here, only winding approaches to conclusions, but the endless search for knowledge has been an exceptionally happy one. The same, dear fellow students, to you.

CONTENTS

	Page
Foreword	v
Love Under the Republicans (or Democrats)	1
A Word to Busybodies	2
That Reminds Me	3
Song for Pier Something Or Other	5
Absence Makes the Heart Grow Heart Trouble	7
Always Marry an April Girl	9
Aside to Husbands	10
A Lady Thinks She Is Thirty	11
I Do, I Will, I Have	13
Confession to Be Traced on a Birthday Cake	15
What Almost Every Woman Knows Sooner or Later	17
Tin Wedding Whistle	19
Just Wrap It Up, and I'll Throw It Away Later	21
If Anything Should Arise, It Isn't I	23
Don't Even Tell Your Wife, Particularly	25
Apartment to Sublet — Unfurnished	26
You Have More Freedom in a House	29
I'm Sure She Said Six-Thirty	32
To a Lady Passing Time Better Left Unpassed	34
I Never Even Suggested It	36
Don't Be Cross, Amanda	38
The Nymph and the Shepherd, *or* She Went That-a-way	40
The Strange Case of Mr. Ormantude's Bride	42
A Warning to Wives	43
The Perfect Husband	45

	Page
A Word About Winter	46
Summer Serenade	48
The Strange Case of Mr. Palliser's Palate	49
The Voice of Experience	51
The Solitude of Mr. Powers	53
How to Harry a Husband *or* Is That Accessory Really Nessary?	55
To My Valentine	57
Thoughts Thought on an Avenue	58
The Trouble with Women is Men	59
A Word to Husbands	61
The Unselfish Husband	62
They Won't Believe, on New Year's Eve, That New Year's Day Will Come What May	64
The Anniversary	66
It's About Time	68
How Can Echo Answer What Echo Cannot Hear?	70
Frailty, Thy Name is Misnomer	72
The Middle	74
How to Be Married Without a Spouse, *or* Mr. Kipling, What Have You Done With Mr. Hauksbee?	75
The Strange Case of Mr. Donnybrook's Boredom	77
My Dream	80
Don't Wait, Hit Me Now!	81
The Winner	83
Come On In, the Senility Is Fine	84
Crossing the Border	86
Once More to My Valentine	87

Love under the
Republicans
(or Democrats)

Come live with me and be my love
And we will all the pleasures prove
Of a marriage conducted with economy
In the Twentieth Century Anno Donomy.
We'll live in a dear little walk-up flat
With practically room to swing a cat
And a potted cactus to give it hauteur
And a bathtub equipped with dark brown water.
We'll eat, without undue discouragement,
Foods low in cost but high in nouragement
And quaff with pleasure, while chatting wittily,
The peculiar wine of Little Italy.
We'll remind each other it's smart to be thrifty
And buy our clothes for something-fifty.
We'll bus for miles on holidays
For seats at depressing matinees,
And every Sunday we'll have a lark
And take a walk in Central Park.
And one of these days not too remote
You'll probably up and cut my throat.

A Word to Busybodies

You cannot cure the lovelorn lover's insomnia
By shouting at him, AMOR VINCIT OMNIA

That Reminds Me

Just imagine yourself seated on a shadowy terrace,
And beside you is a girl who stirs you more strangely
    than an heiress.
It is a summer evening at its most superb,
And the moonlight reminds you that To Love is an
    active verb,
And your hand clasps hers, which rests there without
    shrinking,
And after a silence fraught with romance you ask her
    what she is thinking,
And she starts and returns from the moon-washed
    distances to the shadowy veranda,
And says, Oh I was wondering how many bamboo shoots
    a day it takes to feed a baby Giant Panda.
Or you stand with her on a hilltop and gaze on a winter
    sunset,
And everything is as starkly beautiful as a page from
    Sigrid Undset,
And your arm goes around her waist and you make an
    avowal which for masterfully marshaled emotional
    content might have been a page of Ouida's or
    Thackeray's,
And after a silence fraught with romance she says, I
    forgot to order the limes for the Daiquiris.
Or in a twilight drawing room you have just asked the
    most momentous of questions,

3

And after a silence fraught with romance she says, I think
    this little table would look better where that little
    table is, but then where would that little table go,
    have you any suggestions?

And that's the way they go around hitting below our
    belts;

It isn't that nothing is sacred to them, it's just that at
    the Sacred Moment they are always thinking of
    something else.

Song for Pier Something
Or Other

Steamer, steamer, outward bound,
Couldn't you, wouldn't you turn around?
Mightn't you double on your track?
Mightn't you possibly bring her back?
No, says the steamer, no, no, no!
We go, says the steamer, go, go go!
Who, says the steamer, who are you?
Boo! says the steamer.
Boo!

Steamer, steamer, are you sure
You can carry her secure?
Emerge from ice and storm and fog
With an uneventful log?
Chance, says the steamer, I am chance!
Chance, says the steamer, that's romance!
Who, says the steamer, who are you?
Boo! says the steamer.
Boo!

Steamer, steamer, hard and splendid,
Goddess unwittingly offended,
Are the males who prowl your decks
Attractive to the other sex?
Wait, says the steamer, sit and wait.
Fate, says the steamer, I am Fate.
Who, says the steamer, who are you?
Boo! says the steamer.
Boo!

Steamer, cogitate awhile
Before you smile your final smile,
Seven days are yours to mock;
Steamer, wait until you dock.
Wait till she is safe ashore,
Steamer I do not adore!
Boo, says the steamer, and double boo!
Who, says the steamer,
Are you?

Steamer, steamer, I am he
Whose *raison d'être* you bore to sea.
Steamer, lightly you weighed your anchor,
Try so lightly to weigh my rancor.
As soon as she is safely off you
I'll curse you from Sandy Hook to Corfu.

You who carried her off so boldly
Shall pay for it hotly, pay for it coldly,
With fog and howling hurricanes,
And icebergs in the shipping lanes,
And strikes of longshoremen and tugs,
And a passenger list of jitter bugs —
Pooh! says the steamer. Pooh for you!
Toodle-de-oodle-de-oo!

Absence Makes the Heart
Grow Heart Trouble

I know a girl who is in Paris, France,
And I fear that every evening she goes out to dance,
And she ought to be pining for the undersigned,
But I fear that nothing is further from her mind,
And what is very suspicious, her letters say that she is
    being very quiet,
But my nerves deny it,
And I am unhappily sure that she is drinking champagne
    with aristocrats,
And exchanging cynicisms with sophistocrats.
She goes walking in the Bois
With elegant young men who are not *moi*.
She is receiving compliments from ambassadors,
And riding in *fiacres* with foreign agents who cry that
    for her they would betray the secrets of their lords
    and massadors.
Artists and symphony conductors tempt her with their
    entire repertoire from *Pagliacci to Götterdäm-*
    merung;
Argentines and Brazilians
Seek to dazzle her with their dazzling millions;

Men of the world with etchings and monocles

Plead with her to become part of their personal chronicles;

Aides and equerries try to explain without too much bluntness and yet without too much shyness

The advantages a girl or a tailor enjoys when he or she is entitled to the subtitle of By Appointment to His Royal Highness.

Trips abroad are very nice for Davis Cup teams and Olympic teams, and that's about all you can say for them,

Because I think that when you are fond of somebody you would rather be with them than away from them,

So I wish that time would suddenly advance,

Because I want to be standing on the dock trying to find somebody on deck who will undoubtedly be wearing a terribly smart and perfectly terrible hat which she bought in Paris, France.

Always Marry
an April Girl

Praise the spells and bless the charms,
I found April in my arms.
April golden, April cloudy,
Gracious, cruel, tender, rowdy;
April soft in flowered languor,
April cold with sudden anger,
Ever changing, ever true —
I love April, I love you.

Aside to Husbands

What do you do when you've wedded a girl all legal and
lawful,

And she goes around saying she looks awful?

When she makes deprecatory remarks about her format,

And claims that her hair looks like a doormat?

When she swears that the complexion of which you are
so fond

Looks like the bottom of a dried-up pond?

When she for whom your affection is not the least like
Plato's

Compares her waist to a badly tied sack of potatoes?

Oh, who wouldn't rather be on a flimsy bridge with a
hungry lion at one end and a hungry tiger at the
other end and hungry crocodiles underneath

Than confronted by their dearest making remarks about
her own appearance through clenched teeth?

Why won't they believe that the reason they find themselves the mother of your children is because you
think of all the looks in the world, their looks are
the nicest?

Why must we continue to be thus constantly ordealed
and crisised?

I think it high time these hoity-toity ladies were made to
realize that when they impugn their face and their
ankles and their waist

They are thereby insultingly impugning their tasteful
husbands' impeccable taste.

A Lady Thinks She is Thirty

Unwillingly Miranda wakes,
Feels the sun with terror,
One unwilling step she takes,
Shuddering to the mirror.

Miranda in Miranda's sight
Is old and gray and dirty;
Twenty-nine she was last night;
This morning she is thirty.

Shining like the morning star,
Like the twilight shining,
Haunted by a calendar,
Miranda sits a-pining.

Silly girl, silver girl,
Draw the mirror toward you;
Time who makes the years to whirl
Adorned as he adored you.

Time is timelessness for you;
Calendars for the human;
What's a year, or thirty, to
Loveliness made woman?

Oh, Night will not see thirty again,
Yet soft her wing, Miranda;
Pick up your glass and tell me, then —
How old is Spring, Miranda?

I Do, I Will, I Have

How wise I am to have instructed the butler to instruct
    the first footman to instruct the second footman to
    instruct the doorman to order my carriage;
I am about to volunteer a definition of marriage.
Just as I know that there are two Hagens, Walter and
    Copen,
I know that marriage is a legal and religious alliance
    entered into by a man who can't sleep with the
    window shut and a woman who can't sleep with the
    window open.
Moreover, just as I am unsure of the difference between
    flora and fauna and flotsam and jetsam,
I am quite sure that marriage is the alliance of two people
    one of whom never remembers birthdays and the
    other never forgetsam,
And he refuses to believe there is a leak in the water pipe
    or the gas pipe and she is convinced she is about to
    asphyxiate or drown,
And she says, Quick get up and get my hairbrushes off
    the window sill, it's raining in, and he replies, Oh
    they're all right, its only raining straight down.
That is why marriage is so much more interesting than
    divorce,
Because it's the only known example of the happy meet-
    ing of the immovable object and the irresistible force.

So I hope husbands and wives will continue to debate and combat over everything debatable and combatable. Because I believe a little incompatibility is the spice of life, particularly if he has income and she is pattable.

Confession to be Traced
on a Birthday Cake

Lots of people are richer than me,
Yet pay a slenderer tax;
Their annual levy seems to wane
While their income seems to wax.
Lots of people have stocks and bonds
To further their romances;
I've cashed my ultimate Savings Stamp —
But nobody else has Frances.

Lots of people are stronger than me,
And greater athletic menaces;
They poise like gods on diving boards
And win their golfs and tennises.
Lots of people have lots more grace
And cut fine figures at dances,
While I was born with galoshes on —
But nobody else has Frances.

Lots of people are wiser than me,
And carry within their cranium
The implications of Stein and Joyce
And the properties of uranium.
They know the mileage of every star
In the heaven's vast expanses;
I'm inclined to believe that the world is flat —
But nobody else has Frances.

Speaking of wisdom and wealth and grace —
As recently I have dared to —
There are lots of people compared to whom
I'd rather not be compared to.
There are people I ought to wish I was;
But under the circumstances,
I prefer to continue my life as me —
For nobody else has Frances.

What Almost Every
Woman Knows
Sooner or Later

Husbands are things that wives have to get used to
    putting up with,
And with whom they breakfast with and sup with.
They interfere with the discipline of nurseries,
And forget anniversaries,
And when they have been particularly remiss
They think they can cure everything with a great big
    kiss,
And when you tell them about something they have
    done they just look unbearably patient and smile
    a superior smile,
And think, Oh she'll get over it after a while.
And they always drink cocktails faster than they can
    assimilate them,
And if you look in their direction they act as if they
    were martyrs and you were trying to sacrifice, or
    immolate them.
And they never want to get up or go to bed at the same
    time as you do,
And when you perform some simple rite like putting cold
    cream on your face or applying a touch of lipstick
    they seem to think you are up to some kind of black
    magic like a priestess of Voodoo,
And they are brave and calm and cool and collected about
    the ailments of the person they have promised to
    honor and cherish,

But the minute they get a sniffle or a stomachache of
their own, why you'd think they were about to perish,

And when you are alone with them they ignore all the
minor courtesies, and as for airs and graces they
utterly lack them,

But when there are a lot of people around they hand you
so many chairs and ashtrays and sandwiches and
butter you with such bowings and scrapings that
you want to smack them.

Husbands are indeed an irritating form of life,

And yet through some quirk of Providence most of them
are really very deeply ensconced in the affection of
their wife.

Tin Wedding Whistle

Though you know it anyhow
Listen to me, darling, now,

Proving what I need not prove,
How I know I love you, love.

Near and far, near and far,
I am happy where you are;

Likewise I have never larnt
How to be it where you aren't.

Far and wide, far and wide,
I can walk with you beside;

Furthermore, I tell you what,
I sit and sulk where you are not.

Visitors remark my frown
When you're upstairs and I am down,

In fact I care not where you be,
Just as long as it's with me.

In all your absences I glimpse
Fire and flood and trolls and imps.

Is your train a minute slothful?
I goad the stationmaster wrothful.

When with friends to bridge you drive
I never know if you're alive,

And when you linger late in shops
I long to telephone the cops.

Yet how worth the waiting for,
To see you coming through the door.

Somehow, I can be complacent
Never but with you adjacent.

Near and far, near and far,
I am happy where you are;

Likewise, I have never larnt
How to be it where you aren't.

Then grudge me not my fond endeavor,
To hold you in my sight forever;

Yes, and I'm afraid I pout
When I'm indoors and you are out;

But how contentedly I view
Any room containing you.

Let none, not even you, disparage
Such valid reason for a marriage.

Just Wrap It Up, and
I'll Throw It Away Later

Men think that men have more sense than women and
    women think that any woman has more sense than
    any man,

An issue which I eagerly evade, for who am I to pass
    judgment on the comparative reasoning processes
    of, say, Mr. Lunt and Miss Fontanne?

However, I ask you to visualize, please, a clear-thinking
    American male who needs a hat, or a left sock, or
    an ashtray in the form of the statue Civic Virtue by
    the sculptor MacMonnies,

And what does he do, he goes into the likeliest shop and
    buys it and returns to the regular evening race with
    the children for first go at the funnies.

Kindly contrast this with the procedure of his wife or
sister or aunt who drops into a store for three ounces
of flax for the spinning wheel or an extra minuet
for the spinet,

And what happens, the doorstep is crawling for days with
people delivering lampshades and bedspreads and
dirndls and chairs that expand into bridge tables and
bridge tables that expand into chaises longues, and
husbands who can't bear it simply have to grin it.

Man's idea of shopping is to buy what he needs and get
through with it.

Woman's idea is to have everything she has never needed
sent home and then figure out what to do with it.

It is as true today as in the day of David and Goliath or
Corbett and Fitzsimmons,

That men go into a shop to supply a want, and women
principally to stimulate their imaginations, but
men's imaginations need no extra stimulus as long
as their world is filled with beautiful unanswerable
womens.

If Anything Should Arise,
It Isn't I

A prepared position Man hankers for
Is parallel to and above the floor,
For thither retreating horizontally,
He avades the issues that charge him frontally.
But pumpkins do not burgeon in Maytime,
And bed is out of bounds in daytime.
A man in pyjamas after nine
Transgresses the housewife's Party Line.
He's unethical and unpatriotic,
Unkempt, uncouth, unaristocrotic,
Unwept, unhonored, unsung, unread,
And, if he doesn't get up, unfed.
That is why he smiles when the moment comes
When hands are hot and forehead hums,
When throat is parched and nostrils rankle
And legs are aching from knee to ankle.
Making sure the housewife observes his plight,
He bravely whispers he's all right,
What's a spot of fever, a spell of dizziness.
Where's his hat, he is off to business.
So she telephones the office for him,
And stoups of lemonade doth pour him,
And trees his shoes and hangs his clothes up
And introduces drops his nose up,

She fetches toast as light as froth,
And bouillon, consommé and broth.
And be he Harvardite or Yaleite,
She orders him to bed by daylight,
Like Heaven chastening a Baalite
She orders him to bed by daylight.
Beneath the sheets he cracks his knuckles
And chokes to cover up his chuckles,
And coughs a spirited cadenza
In grateful praise of influenza.

Don't Even Tell Your
Wife, Particularly

All good men believe that women would rather get rid
    of a piece of gossip than a bulge,

And all good women believe that gossip is a feminine
    weakness in which men never indulge.

Rather than give ear to scandalous rumors,

Why, men would rather play golf in bloomers,

And rather than talk behind each other's backs,

They would go shopping in a mink coat and slacks.

It is one of each sex's uniquenesses

That men's talk is all of humanity's aspirations, and
    women's all of their friends' weaknesses.

Yes, this is a universal credo that no amount of evidence
    can alter,

Including that of Petronius, Suetonius, Pepys, Boswell,
    the locker room of the country club, and Mrs.
    Winchell's little boy, Walter.

Allow me to ask and answer one question before depart-
    ing for Mount Everest or Lake Ossipee:

Who says men aren't gossipy? — Men say men aren't
    gossipy.

Apartment to Sublet—
Unfurnished

The Murrays are hunting a house,
They are tired of living in flats.
They long for a personal mouse
And a couple of personal cats.
They are hunting a house to inhabit,
An Eden, or even an Arden,
They are thinking of keeping a rabbit,
They are thinking of digging a garden.
How giddy the Murrays have grown
To aspire to a house of their own!

Oh, hurry, hurry!
Says Mrs. Murray.
Tarry awhile, says he,
If you care for a house
As is a house,
You'd better leave it to me.
I'd like an orchard, apple or peach,
I'd like an accessible bathing beach,
And a den for unwinding detective plots,
And a lawn for practising mashie shots,
And open fires,
And a pleasant sunroom,

A handy garage,
And perhaps a gunroom,
And an atmosphere exempt of static,
And a furnace silent and automatic.
For such a house
I would hurry, hurry —
I'm a practical man,
Says Mr. Murray.

The Murrays of 17 B,
The Murrays are going away
From the wireless in 17 C,
And the parties in 17 A.
For the Murrays are tired of flats,
They are rapidly growing aloof
As they dream of their personal cats,
As they dream of their personal roof.
Their friends cannot smother their merriment
When they speak of the Murrays' experiment.

Oh, hurry, hurry!
Says Mr. Murray.
Tarry awhile, says she.
When we choose a house,
Let us choose a house
As nice as a house can be.
With a dozen windows south and east,
And a dozen capacious cupboards at least,
And a laundry lilting with light and air,

And a porch for a lady to dry her hair,
And plenty of sun,
And plenty of shade,
And a neat little place
For a possible maid,
And a wall with roses clambering wild,
And a quiet room for a sleepy child.
If you happen to see it,
Hurry, hurry!
For *that's* the house,
Says Mrs. Murray.

You Have More Freedom
in a House

The Murrays are snug in their house,
They are finished forever with flats;
They longed for a personal mouse
And room to swing dozens of cats.
They longed for a hearth and a doorway,
In Arden, or maybe in Eden,
But the Eden is rather like Norway,
And the Arden like winter in Sweden.
How baffled the Murrays have grown
Since they live in a house of their own!

Oh, hurry, hurry!
Says Mrs. Murray.
But listen, my dear, says he,
If you want the house
A temperate house,
You'd better not leave it to me.
I've learned the knack of swinging a cat,
But I can't coerce the thermostat.
The furnace has given a gruesome cough,
And something has cut the fuel off,
And the heart of the nursery radiator
Is cold as the prose of Walter Pater,
And I've telephoned for the service men

But they can't get here until after ten,
So swaddle the children
And hurry, hurry —
I'm a practical man,
Says Mr. Murray.

The Murrays are vague about fuses
And mechanical matters like that,
And each of them frequently muses
On the days when they lived in a flat.
Was the plumbing reluctant to plumb?
Was the climate suggestive of Canada?
Did the radio crackle and hum?
You simply called down to the janitor!
The Murrays have found no replacement
For the genius who lived in the basement.

Oh, hurry, hurry!
Says Mr. Murray.
I'm doing my best, says she,
But it's hard to scrub
In a tepid tub,
So the guests must wait for me;
And tell them they'll get their cocktails later
When you've managed to fix the refrigerator.
And explain if the coffee looks like water
That the stove is as queer as a seventh daughter,
And I will be down as soon as able
To unstick the drawers of my dressing table.

There's a car at the door, says Mrs. Murray,
The doorbell's broken, so hurry, hurry!
Oh, I don't regret
Being wed to you,
But I wish I could wed
A janitor too.

I'm Sure She Said
Six-Thirty

One of the hardest explanations to be found
Is an explanation for just standing around.
Anyone just standing around looks pretty sinister,
Even a minister;
Consider then the plight of the criminal,
Who lacks even the protective coloration of a hymnal,
And as just standing around is any good criminal's
    practically daily stint,
I wish to proffer a hint.
Are you, sir, a masher who blushes as he loiters,
Do you stammer to passersby that you are merely expect-
    ing a streetcar, or a dispatch from Reuter's?
      Or perhaps you are a safeblower engaged in casing
      a joint;
Can you look the patrolman in the eye or do you forget
    all the savoir-faire you ever loint?
Suppose you are a shoplifter awaiting an opportunity to
    lift a shop,
Or simply a novice with a length of lead pipe killing time
    in a dark alley pending the arrival of a wealthy fop,
Well, should any official ask you why you are just stand-
    ing around,
Do you wish you could simply sink into the ground?

My dear sir, do not be embarrassed, do not reach for your
    gun or your knife,
Remember the password, which, uttered in a tone of quiet
    despair, is the explanation of anyone's standing
    around anywhere at any hour for any length of time:
    "I'm waiting for my wife."

To a Lady Passing Time
Better Left Unpassed

O lady of the lucent hair,
Why do you play at solitaire?
What imp, what demon misanthrope,
Prompted this session of lonely hope?
What boredom drives you, and great Lord!
How can such as you be bored?
The gleaming world awaits your eye
While you essay futility.
That mouth is shaped for livelier sport
Than paging of a pasteboard court —
Why, even the Red Knave longing lingers,
While Black Queens wait, in those white fingers.
See now the joy that lights your face
Squandered on some fortuitous ace,
Where formerly dark anger burned
When a five perverse would not be turned.
O, know you not, that darkling frown
Could topple Caesar's empire down;
That quick, bright joy, if flashed on men,
Could sudden build it up again?
Get up! Get up! Throw down the pack!
Rise in your gown of shining black!
Withdraw, my dear, while you are able
The slender feet from 'neath the table;
Remove from the regretful baize
The elbows curved in cunning ways.

Is there no game that pleasure brings
But fretting over painted things?
No gay, ecstatic end in view
But shuffle and begin anew?
Get up, I tell you, girl, get up!
Wine keeps not ever in the cup;
Music is mortal, comes a day
When the musicians will not play;
Even love immortal, love undying,
Finds the loved one's Patience trying.
Let two-and-fifty rivals hiss me —
For God's sake, girl, come here and kiss me!

I Never Even Suggested It

I know lots of men who are in love and lots of men who
    are married and lots of men who are both,
And to fall out with their loved ones is what all of them
    are most loth.
They are conciliatory at every opportunity,
Because all they want is serenity and a certain amount
    of impunity.
Yes, many the swain who has finally admitted that the
    earth is flat
Simply to sidestep a spat,
Many the masculine Positively or Absolutely which has
    been diluted to an If
Simply to avert a tiff,
Many the two-fisted executive whose domestic conversa-
    tion is limited to a tactfully interpolated Yes,
And then he is amazed to find that he is being raked
    backwards over a bed of coals nevertheless.
These misguided fellows are under the impression that
    it takes two to make a quarrel, that you can sidestep
    a crisis by nonaggression and nonresistance,
Instead of removing yourself to a discreet distance.
Passivity can be a provoking modus operandi;
Consider the Empire and Gandhi.
Silence is golden, but sometimes invisibility is golder,

Because loved ones may not be able to make bricks without straw, but often they don't need any straw to
manufacture a bone to pick or a chip for their soft
white shoulder.
It is my duty, gentlemen, to inform you that women are
dictators all, and I recommend to you this moral:
In real life it takes only one to make a quarrel.

Don't Be Cross, Amanda

Don't be cross, Amanda,
Amanda, don't be cross,
For when you're cross, Amanda,
I feel an albatross
Around my neck, or dank gray moss,
And my eyes assume an impervious gloss.
Amanda,
Dear Amanda,
Don't be cross.

Do not frown, Amanda,
Amanda, do not frown,
For when you frown, Amanda,
I wamble like a clown,
My mouth is stuffed with eiderdown,
And I spatter coffee upon your gown.
Amanda,
Dear Amanda,
Do not frown.

Don't clam up, Amanda,
Amanda, do not clam,
For when you clam, Amanda,
I don't know where I am.
What is it that I did you damn?

Shall I make amends for a sheep, or a lamb?
Amanda,
Dear Amanda,
Do not clam.

Please be gay, Amanda,
Amanda, please be gay,
For when you're gay, Amanda,
The stars come out by day,
The police throw parking tags away,
And I want to kick up my heels and bray.
Amanda,
Dear Amanda,
Please be gay.

The Nymph and the
Shepherd
OR
She Went That-a-way

Few things are less endearing than a personal comparison,
But I know a lady who is very like the elusive mother of
    Mr. Milne's James James Morrison Morrison.
She would be a perfect wife could she but be restrained
    by a leash or a fetter,
Because she has the roving tendencies of an Irish setter.
Her husband assists her from the cab and stops to pay
    the fare,
And when he turns around she isn't there,
She is a hundred yards off, blithe as a flock of linnets,
And in a fair way to do the mile under four minutes.
He assists her from the train and by the time he has
    caught a porter she is at the top of the moving
    stairway,
And again to do the mile under four minutes she is in
    a fair way.
She shoots ahead of him in London crowds and leaves
    him behind fumbling with lire in Pisa,
Despite the fact that he is in sole possession of all the
    travelers' checks and their joint passport and visa.
If in the Louvre she exclaims, "Oh, look at the Mona
    Lisa!" and he pauses to look at the Mona Lisa,

By the time he has looked she is three corners and forty
  masterpieces away, and himself alone with the same
  old money and passport and visa.
Sometimes he is touched and flattered by her faith in
  him, but mostly he feels like Queen Victoria's chair,
Which Queen Victoria never looked behind at before she
  sat down, because she just knew it would be there.

The Strange Case of
Mr. Ormantude's Bride

Once there was a bridegroom named Mr. Ormantude
    whose intentions were hard to disparage,
Because he intended to make his a happy marriage,
And he succeeded for going on fifty years,
During which he was in marital bliss up to his ears.
His wife's days and nights were enjoyable
Because he catered to every foible;
He went around humming hymns
And anticipating her whims.
Many a fine bit of repartee died on his lips
Lest it throw her anecdotes into eclipse;
He was always silent when his cause was meritorious,
And he never engaged in argument unless sure he was
    so obviously wrong that she couldn't help emerging
    victorious,
And always when in her vicinity
He was careful to make allowances for her femininity;
Were she snappish, he was sweetish,
And of understanding her he made a fetish.
Everybody said his chances of celebrating his golden
    wedding looked good,
But on his golden wedding eve he was competently
    poisoned by his wife who could no longer stand being
    perpetually understood.

A Warning to Wives

Speak gently to your husband, ma'am,
And encourage all his sneezes;
That nasty cough may carry him off
If exposed to drafts and breezes.
But suppose the scoundrel lingers on
And insists on being cured;
Well, it isn't a sin if a girl steps in —
Unless the brute's insured.

Oh the selfishness of men, welladay, welladay!
Oh the sissies, oh the softies, oh the mice!
Egotistically they strive to keep themselves alive,
And insurance is their scurviest device.
Insurance!
It's insurance
That tries a lady's temper past endurance.
Yet it's safer, on the whole,
To practice self-control
If there's apt to be a question of insurance.

Arsenic soup is a dainty soup,
But not if he's paid his premium.
Or a ·32 in a pinch will do,
If you're bored with the epithalemium.

But to make acquittal doubly sure —
No maybes, no perhapses —
You'll do well to wait to expunge your mate
Until his policy lapses.

The hypocrisy of men, welladay, welladay!
Whited sepulchers are much to be preferred.
They claim it's for their wives they evaluate their
    lives,
But it's fatal if you take them at their word.
Insurance!
Oh insurance!
What holds potential widows fast in durance?
Not the Adlers and the Freuds,
But the Mutuals and Lloyds,
And the jury's evil mind about insurance.

The Perfect Husband

He tells you when you've got on too much lipstick,
And helps you with your girdle when your hips stick.

A Word About Winter

Now the frost is on the pane,
Rugs upon the floor again,
Now the screens are in the cellar,
Now the student cons the speller,
Lengthy summer noon is gone,
Twilight treads the heels of dawn,
Round-eyed sun is now a squinter,
Tiptoe breeze a panting sprinter,
Every cloud a blizzard hinter,
Squirrel on the snow a printer,
Rainspout sprouteth icy splinter,
Willy-nilly, this is winter.

Summer-swollen doorjambs settle,
Ponds and puddles turn to metal,
Skater whoops in frisky fettle,
Golf club stingeth like a nettle,
Radiator sings like kettle,
Hearth is Popocatepetl.

Runneth nose and chappeth lip,
Draft evadeth weather strip,
Doctor wrestleth with grippe
In never-ending rivalship.
Rosebush droops in garden shoddy,
Blood is cold and thin in body,

Weary postman dreams of toddy,
Head before the hearth grows noddy.

On the hearth the embers gleam,
Glowing like a maiden's dream,
Now the apple and the oak
Paint the sky with chimney smoke,
Husband now, without disgrace,
Dumps ashtrays in the fireplace.

Summer Serenade

When the thunder stalks the sky,
When tickle-footed walks the fly,
When shirt is wet and throat is dry,
Look, my darling, that's July.

Though the grassy lawn be leather,
And prickly temper tug the tether,
Shall we postpone our love for weather?
If we must melt, let's melt together!

The Strange Case of
Mr. Palliser's Palate

Once there was a man named Mr. Palliser and he asked
    his wife, May I be a gourmet?

And she said, You sure may,

But she also said, If my kitchen is going to produce a
    Cordon Blue,

It won't be me, it will be you,

And he said, You mean *Cordon Bleu?*

And she said to never mind the pronunciation so long as
    it was him and not *heu.*

But he wasn't discouraged; he bought a white hat and
    The Cordon Bleu Cook Book and said, How about
    some *Huîtres en Robe de Chambre?*

And she sniffed and said, Are you reading a cook book
    or *Forever Ambre?*

And he said, Well, if you prefer something more Anglo-
    Saxon,

Why suppose I whip up some tasty *Filets de Sole Jackson,*

And she pretended not to hear, so he raised his voice and
    said, Could I please you with some *Paupiettes de
    Veau à la Grecque* or *Cornets de Jambon Lucullus*
    or perhaps some nice *Moules à la Bordelaise?*

And she said, Kindly lower your voice or the neighbors
    will think we are drunk and disordelaise,

And she said, Furthermore the whole idea of your cook-
    ing anything fit to eat is a farce. So what did Mr.
    Palliser do then?

Well, he offered her *Oeufs Farcis Maison* and *Homard
  Farci St. Jacques* and *Tomate Farcie à la Bayonne*
  and *Aubergines Farcies Provençales,* as well as
  Aubergines Farcies Italiennes,
And she said, Edward, kindly accompany me as usual
  to Hamburger Heaven and stop playing the fool,
And he looked in the book for one last suggestion and it
  suggested *Croques Madame,* so he did, and now he
  dines every evening on *Crème de Concombres
  Glacée, Côtelettes de Volaille Vicomtesse,* and
  Artichauds à la Barigoule.

The Voice of Experience

A husband at a lecture
Twitches his architecture.

He undergoes the lecturing
Like unanesthetized vivisecturing.

He's a glassy-eyed conjecturer
Of the ancestry of the lecturer.

Husbands hide in storerooms
To escape Town Halls and Forums.

They improvise In Memoriams
For speakers in auditoriums.

They regard as nauseous nostrums
Opinions delivered from rostrums.

They feel about orators' rhetorics
Like Caesar about Vercingetorix.

They flinch as the fog of boredom
Creeps verbosely toredom.

There is none so irate and awkward
As a husband being Chautauquard.

Their collars grow more and more cumbersome
And at last they essay to slumber some.

But this respite their spouses grudge them,
And if they nod, they nudge them.

The Solitude of
Mr. Powers

Once there was a lonely man named Mr. Powers.

He was lonely because his wife fixed flowers.

Mr. Powers was a gallant husband, but whenever he wished to demonstrate his gal*lan*try

His beloved was always out with six vases and a bunch of something or other in the pantry.

He got no conversation while they ate

Because she was always nipping dead blossoms off the centerpiece and piling them on her plate.

He could get no conversation after meals because if he happened to begin one

She would look at the mantel and wonder if she shouldn't switch the small fat vase with the tall thin one.

Yes, even when she wasn't actually fixing flowers there was no forgetting about them,

Because before fixing them she was busy cutting them, and after fixing them she was busy fretting about them.

Mr. Powers began to shave only once a week because no one cared whether his chin was scratchy;

He felt as lonely as *Cavalleria* without *Pagliacci*.

Finally he said Hey!

I might as well be alone with myself as alone with a lot of vases that have to have their water replenished every day.

And he walked off into the dawn.

And his wife just kept on refilling vases and never noticed
that he was gone.
Beware of floral arrangements;
They lead to marital estrangements.

How to Harry a Husband
OR
Is That Accessory Really Nessary?

Husband stands at door of flat,
Coat in elbow, hand on hat,
In his pocket, from broker shady,
Two good seats for *My Fair Lady*.
Patiently he stands there humming,
Coming, darling? Darling, coming?

But she's a freak and she's a hag,
She's got the wrong, she murmurs, bag,
She's got, she adds in wild distress,
To change the bag or change the dress.
She'd as soon appear with stockings ragged
As be seen incongruously bebaggèd.

Husband rings the bell for lift,
Hears it chunk and upward drift,
Well knows taxis in the rain
Rarer than the whooping crane.
Impatiently he stands there snarling,
Darling, coming? Coming, darling?

Another bag at last she chooses
And everything in the first bag loses.
She fumbles with many a dainty curse
For lipstick, glasses, keys, and purse.*
He grunts, as dies preprandial liquor,
To change from the skin out would have been
    quicker.

They disrupt the middle of the show,
Their seats are middle of the row,
They crawl and climb like tandem tractors
Between the audience and the actors,
Whose delicious rapport might have lagged
Had she been incongruously bebagged.

* Then—
She turns it inside out and scratches
For handkerchief, cigarettes, and matches,
Tweezers, compact, and aspirin,
And Band-Aids redolent of My Sin,
Driver's license and Charga-Plate,
A sweepstake ticket one year late,
A colored chart of a five-day diet,
A Penguin commended by Gilbert Highet,
A tearful appeal from a charitymonger,
And a catalogue from Lewis & Conger.
This is she whose eyes start from their sockets
At the contents of her small son's pockets.

To My Valentine

More than a catbird hates a cat,
Or a criminal hates a clue,
Or an odalisque hates the Sultan's mates,
That's how much I love you.

I love you more than a duck can swim,
And more than a grapefruit squirts,
I love you more than commercials are a bore,
And more than a toothache hurts.

As a shipwrecked sailor hates the sea,
Or a juggler hates a shove,
As a hostess detests unexpected guests,
That's how much you I love.

I love you more than a wasp can sting,
And more than the subway jerks,
I love you truer than a toper loves a brewer,
And more than a hangnail irks.

I love you more than a bronco bucks,
Or a Yale man cheers the Blue.
Ask not what is this thing called love;
It's what I'm in with you.

Thoughts Thought
on an Avenue

There would be far less masculine gaming and boozing
But for the feminine approach to feminine fashions,
   which is distinctly confusing.
Please correct me if, although I don't think I do, I err;
But it is a fact that a lady wants to be dressed exactly
   like everybody else but she gets pretty upset if she
   sees anybody else dressed exactly like her.
Nothing so infuriates her as a similar hat or dress,
Especially if bought for less,
Which brings up another point which I will attempt to
   discuss in my guttural masculine jargon:
Her ideal raiment is costlier than her or her dearest
   friend's purse can buy, and at the same time her own
   exclusive and amazing bargain.
Psychologists claim that men are the dreamers and
   women are the realists,
But to my mind women are the starriest-eyed of idealists,
Though I am willing to withdraw this charge and gladly
   eat it uncomplaineously
If anyone can explain to me how a person can wear a
   costume that is different from other people's and
   the same as other peoples, and more expensive than
   other people's and cheaper than other people's,
   simultaneously.

The Trouble with
Women is Men

A husband is a man who two minutes after his head
    touches the pillow is snoring like an overloaded
    omnibus,
Particularly on those occasions when between the
    humidity and the mosquitoes your own bed is no
    longer a bed but an insomnibus,
And if you turn on the light for a little reading he is
    sensitive to the faintest gleam,
But if by any chance you are asleep and he wakeful, he
    is not slow to rouse you with the complaint that he
    can't close his eyes, what about slipping downstairs
    and freezing him a cooling dish of pistachio ice
    cream.
His touch with a bottle opener is sure,
But he cannot help you get a tight dress over your head
    without catching three hooks and a button in your
    coiffure.
Nor can he so much as wash his ears without leaving an
    inch of water on the bathroom linoleum,
But if you mention it you evoke not a promise to splash
    no more but a mood of deep melancholium.
Indeed, each time he transgresses your chance of cor-
    recting his faults grows lesser,

Because he produces either a maddeningly logical explanation or a look of martyrdom which leaves you instead of him feeling the remorse of the transgressor.

Such are husbandly foibles, but there are moments when a foible ceases to be a foible.

Next time you ask for a glass of water and when he brings it you have a needle almost threaded and instead of setting it down he stands there holding it out to you, just kick him fairly hard in the stomach, you will find it thoroughly enjoible.

A Word to Husbands

To keep your marriage brimming,
With love in the loving cup,
Whenever you're wrong, admit it;
Whenever you're right, shut up.

The Unselfish Husband

Once upon a time there was a man named Orlando
Tregennis and he was in love with his wife,

And he thought he would express his love by serenading
her, but his serenade wasn't very successful because
his playing interfered with his singing because all
he could play was the fife,

So then he said, I will climb the highest mountain in the
world and name it after my wife and then she will
give me a look of love, so he climbed the highest
mountain in the world and his wife was indeed whom
he named it after,

But she didn't give him a look of love, she gave him a
look of laughter,

And not only a look of laughter but a look of menace,

Because he named it after his wife by naming it Mt. Mrs.
Orlando Tregennis,

So then he said that he certainly was sorry that during
the first war he had absentmindedly forgotten to
join the army,

Because he said if he had been entitled to a bonus he
would have given her every penny even though she
was already so entrancing that no amount of mere
money could make her a jot or tittle more allury
or charmy,

And she greeted this remark with ribald merriment,

And she said that possibly money wouldn't get her any
further than she was, but she'd like a chance to try
the experiment,
So then Mr. Tregennis said, Well, I haven't any gold,
But I will give you my most precious possession, I will
give you my cold,
And he gave her his cold and first of all she tried to
spurn it,
And then she tried to return it,
But he said, No, darling, now it's your very own cold,
It is yours to have and to hold,
Because if you reckon I don't give gifts for keeps you
made a mistake when you reckoned,
Because there hasn't been an Indian-giver in the Tre-
gennis family since my great-great-grandfather, old
Hiawatha Tregennis II.
But she wouldn't take no for an answer, but he wouldn't
say yes, and Mr. Tregennis's precious cold went
shuttling back and forth between them for the rest
of their lives,
And I hope everybody will turn out to be such self-
sacrificing husbands and wives.

They Won't Believe,
On New Year's Eve,
That New Year's Day
Will Come What May

How do I feel today? I feel as unfit as an unfiddle,

And it is the result of a certain turbulence in the mind
and an uncertain burbulence in the middle.

What was it anyway, that angry thing that flew at me?

I am unused to banshees crying Boo at me.

Your wife can't be a banshee,

Or can she?

Of course, some wives become less fond

When you're bottled in bond.

My Uncle George, in lavender-scented Aunt Edna's day,

If he had a glass of beer on Saturday night, he didn't dare
come home till the following Wednesday.

I see now that he had hit upon the ideal idea,

The passage of time, and plenty of it, is the only marital
panacea.

Ah, if the passage of time were backward, and last night
I'd been a child again, this morning I'd be fragrant
with orange-juice,

Instead of reeking of pinch-bottle foreign juice;

But if I should turn out to be a child again, what would
life hold for me?

The woman I love would be too old for me.
There's only one solution to my problem, a hair of the
    dog, or maybe a couple of hairs;
Then if she doesn't get mad at me life will be peaceful,
    and if she does it will show she really cares.

The Anniversary

A marriage aged one
Is hardly begun;
A fling in the sun,
But it's hardly begun;
A green horse,
A stiff course,
And leagues to be run.

A marriage aged five
Is coming alive.
Watch it wither and thrive;
Though it's coming alive,
You must guess,
No or yes,
If it's going to survive.

A marriage aged ten
Is a hopeful Amen;
It's pray for it then,
And mutter Amen;
As the names
Of old flames
Sound again and again.

At twenty a marriage
Discovers its courage.
This year do not disparage,
It is comely in courage;

Past the teens
And blue jeans,
It's a promising marriage.

Yet before twenty-one
It has hardly begun.
How tall in the sun,
Yet hardly begun!
But once come of age,
Pragmatically sage,
Oh, blithe to engage
Is sweet marri-age.

Tilt a twenty-first cup
To a marriage grown up,
Now sure and mature,
And securely grown up.
Raise twenty-one cheers
To the silly young years,
While I sit out the dance
With my dearest of dears.

It's About Time

How simple was the relationship between the sexes in
    the days of Francesca di Rimini;
Men were menacing, women were womeny.
When confronted with women, men weren't expected to
    understand them;
Their alternatives were, if accepted, to embrace, if re-
    jected, to unhand them.
I attribute much of our modern tension
To a misguided striving for intersexual comprehension.
It's about time to realize, brethren, as best we can,
That a woman is not just a female man.
How bootless, then, to chafe
When they are late because they have no watch with
    them, all eleven of their watches are on the dressing
    table or in the safe;
How fruitless to pout
Because they believe that every time the dog scratches it
    really wants to go out;
Give your tongue to the cat
When you ask what they want for their birthday and
    they say, Oh anything, and you get anything, and
    then discover it should have been anything but that.
Pocket the gold, fellows, ask not why it glisters;

As Margaret Fuller accepted the universe, so let us
    accept her sisters.
Women would I think be easier nationalized
Than rationalized,
And the battle of the sexes can be a most enjoyable
    scrimmage
If you'll only stop trying to create woman in your
    own image.

How can Echo Answer
What Echo Cannot Hear?

Why shouldn't I laud my love?
My love is highly laudable;
Indeed, she would be perfection
Were she only always audible.

Why shouldn't I laud her voice,
The welcomest sound I know,
Her voice, which is ever soft?
It is likewise gentle and low —

An excellent thing in woman
And the Wilson's thrush, or veery —
But there are maddening moments
When I wish I had wed a Valkyrie.

Whenever her talk is restricted
To topics inconsequential
She utters it face to face,
With clarity reverential.

Then why, when there's something important to say,
Does she always say it going away?
She'll remark, as she mounts the stairs to bed,
"Oh, some FBI man called and said . . ."
Then her words, like birds too swift for banding,

Vanish with her upon the landing.
"Don't you think we ought . . ." Then she's gone, whereat
The conclusion fades out like the Cheshire Cat.
Yes, her words when weighty with joy or dread
Seem to emerge from the back of her head;
The dénouement supreme, the point of the joke,
Is forever drifting away like smoke.
Knowing her custom, knowing the wont of her,
I spend my life circling to get in front of her.

I'll bet that the poet Herrick,
With Corinna gone a-Maying,
Had to run like a rabbit
To catch what she was saying.

Frailty, Thy Name
is a Misnomer

Once there was a couple named Mr. and Mrs. Pepperloaf
and they were simply devoted,
Because each other was upon what they doted,
And in Mrs. Pepperloaf's eyes Mr. Pepperloaf could
never err,
And he admitted only one flaw in her,
But it was a flaw which took many virtues to assuage,
Consisting in always asking him the date while she was
reading the paper with the date clearly printed on
every page,
And whenever he called her attention to this least admir-
able of her traits
She would retort that he didn't trust the paper's weather
forecasts so then why should she trust its dates.
For eleven years his patience held
But finally he rebelled.
It was on the evening of Friday the seventh that she
looked up from her paper and asked him the date,
And he replied firmly that she would find it at the top
of the page, so she looked at the top of the page
and that was that, and presently they sat down to
supper and ate,
And they were miserable because they had never dis-
agreed and this contretemps was a beginner for them,

And at nine his employer's wife called up to ask where
   were they, she and eleven guests were waiting dinner
   for them,
And Mr. Pepperloaf asked Mrs. Pepperloaf how she could
   have so misreckoned,
And she said she knew that they had been invited out on
   the seventh, but according to the newspaper he had
   instructed her to consult tonight was only the second,
And he picked up the paper and it was last week's, not
   today's,
And she said certainly, she had just been keeping it to
   read over some recipes for different delicious soufflés,
And now she found the first flaw in him, because she had
   obeyed his order to look for the date in the paper,
   hadn't she, so his irritation was uncalled for and
   unseasonable.
Women would rather be right than reasonable.

The Middle

When I remember bygone days
I think how evening follows morn;
So many I loved were not yet dead,
So many I love were not yet born.

How to be Married
Without a Spouse
OR
Mr. Kipling, What Have
You Done With
Mr. Hauksbee?

Do any of you old fogies remember Mrs. Hauksbee?
    Without Mrs. Hauksbee, Simla and Poona
Would have been just like Altoona.
At Mrs. Hauksbee's *burra khanas*
Nabobs pinned tails on donkeys and viceroys bobbed for
    bananas.
Mrs. Hauksbee disentangled subalterns and aides-de-
    camp
From shopworn maids-de-camp.
Under the deodars, whatever they may be, Mrs.
    Hauksbee was in her glory,
But this is another story.
Mrs. Hauksbee was attended by a faithful old *amah*,
Which is the equivalent of in Alabama a faithful old
    mamah,
And this now *amah* was a conservative reactionary Hindu,
And she got tired of Mrs. Hauksbee all the time shifting
    her hemline and her hair-do and her skin-do,

And finally she asked Mrs. Hauksbee why she had dyed
　　her hair again and she got one of the usual answers.
Mrs. Hauksbee said she was changing her style to reform
　　young Slingsby of the Umpteenth Lancers,
And the *amah* (she had surreptitiously attended the
　　Sorbonne)
Murmured, *"Plus ça change, plus c'est la memsahib,"* and
　　wandered on.

The Strange Case of
Mr. Donnybrook's
Boredom

Once upon a time there was a man named Mr. Donnybrook.

❧

He was married to a woman named Mrs. Donnybrook.

❧

Mr. and Mrs. Donnybrook dearly loved to be bored.

❧

Sometimes they were bored at the ballet, other times at
the cinema.

❧

They were bored riding elephants in India and elevators
in the Empire State Building.

❧

They were bored in speakeasies during Prohibition and
in cocktail lounges after Repeal.

❧

They were bored by Grand Dukes and garbagemen,
debutantes and demimondaines, opera singers and
Onassises.

❧

They scoured the Five Continents and the Seven Seas in
their mad pursuit of boredom.

❧

This went on for years and years.

❧

One day Mr. Donnybrook turned to Mrs. Donnybrook,

❧

My dear, he said, we have reached the end of our rope.

❧

We have exhausted every yawn.

❧

The world holds nothing more to jade our titillated palates.

❧

Well, said Mrs. Donnybrook, we might try insomnia.

❧

So they tried insomnia.

❧

About two o'clock the next morning Mr. Donnybrook said, My, insomnia is certainly quite boring, isn't it?

❧

Mrs. Donnybrook said it certainly was, wasn't it?

❧

Mr. Donnybrook said it certainly was.

❧

Pretty soon he began to count sheep.

❧

Mrs. Donnybrook began to count sheep, too.

❧

After a while Mr. Donnybrook said, Hey, you're counting my sheep!

❧

Stop counting my sheep, said Mr. Donnybrook.

❧

Why, the very idea, said Mrs. Donnybrook.

❧

I guess I know my own sheep, don't I?

❧

How? said Mr. Donnybrook.

❧

They're cattle, said Mrs. Donnybrook.

❧

They're cattle, and longhorns at that.

❧

Furthermore, said Mrs. Donnybrook, us cattle ranchers
is shore tired o' you sheepmen plumb ruinin' our
water.

❧

I give yuh fair warnin', said Mrs. Donnybrook, yuh better
git them woolly Gila monsters o' yourn back across
the Rio Grande afore mornin' or I'm a-goin' to string
yuh up on the nearest cottonwood.

❧

Carramba! sneered Mr. Donnybrook. Thees ees free
range, no?

❧

No, said Mrs. Donnybrook, not for sheepmen.

❧

She strung him up on the nearest cottonwood.

❧

Mr. Donnybrook had never been so bored in his life.

My Dream

Here is a dream.
It is my dream,
My own dream,
I dreamt it.
I dreamt that my hair was kempt,
Then I dreamt that my true love unkempt it.

Don't Wait, Hit Me Now!

If there are any wives present who wish to irritate their
    husbands or husbands who wish to irritate their
    wives,
Why, I know an irritation more irritating than hives,
So if you think such an irritation expedient,
Here is the formula, in which the presence of a third
    person is the only essential extra ingredient;
Indeed it is beautifully simple,
But it is guaranteed to make a molehill out of a dimple,
And what it consists of is that when you are annoyed
    with your husband or wife and want to do the
    opposite of woo them,
Why, you just talk at them instead of to them.
Suppose you think your Gregory danced too often with
    Mrs. Limbworthy at the club, you don't say to him
    directly, "Gregory, I'll smack you down if you don't
    lay off that platinum-plated hussy,"
No, you wait till a friend drops in and then with a glance
    at Gregory say to her, "Isn't it funny what fools
    middle-aged men can make of themselves over any-
    thing blonde and slithery, do you understand how
    anybody sober and in their right mind could look
    twice at that Limbworthy job, but then of course
    darling, Gregory wasn't altogether in his right mind
    last night, was he?"
This is indeed more excruciating to Gregory than
    Shakespearian excursions and alarums,

Because there is no defense against caroms.

Or let us suppose you are irked by your Esmeralda's sudden passion for antiques,

Well, you don't mention it for weeks,

No, you wait till a friend drops in and then with a glance at Esmeralda you say, "How anybody can be sucked in by this antique racket is beyond me, but there are some otherwise sensible women who'll mortgage their beauty treatments for a genuine secondhand Killarney banshee,

But of course Esmeralda can't ever resist an opportunity to pick up some fossil to amaze her friends with, can she?"

And Esmeralda must sit quiet and take it with apparent docility,

Because the hit direct doesn't compare with the ricochet in deadly unanswerability.

By this easy method can every Gregory score off every Esmeralda and every Esmeralda annihilate every Gregory,

And its only drawback besides eventual divorce is that it reduces all their friends to emotional beggary.

The Winner

Ecstatic poets through the ages
Have writ their love on golden pages,
Treading on one another's toes
Till Bartlett brims and overflows,
And all their memorable phrases
Are common as goldenrod or daisies.
Why should I vie with such, my sweet,
When I descry in you, complete,
That ultimate sonnet, sunset-bright,
That Shakespeare always meant to write?

Come On In,
The Senility is Fine

People live forever in Jackonsville and St. Petersburg and
    Tampa,
But you don't have to live forever to become a grampa.
The entrance requirements for grampahood are com-
    paratively mild,
You only have to live until your child has a child.
From that point on you start looking both ways over your
    shoulder,
Because sometimes you feel thirty years younger and
    sometimes thirty years older.
Now you begin to realize who it was that reached the
    height of imbecility,
It was whoever said that grandparents have all the fun
    and none of the responsibility.
This is the most enticing spiderweb of a tarradiddle ever
    spun,
Because everybody would love to have a baby around
    who was no responsibility and lots of fun,
But I can think of no one but a mooncalf or a gaby
Who would trust their own child to raise a baby.
So you have to personally superintend your grandchild
    from diapers to pants and from bottle to spoon,
Because you know that your own child hasn't sense
    enough to come in out of a typhoon.

You don't have to live forever to become a grampa, but
   if you do want to live forever,
Don't try to be clever;
If you wish to reach the end of the trail with an uncut
   throat,
Don't go around saying Quote I don't mind being a
   grampa but I hate being married to a gramma
   Unquote.

Crossing The Border

Senescence begins
And middle age ends
The day your descendants
Outnumber your friends.

Once More
to My Valentine

Just five and thirty years ago
I walked alone on earth,
That callous, carefree creature,
A bachelor from birth.
No thrill of premonition,
No tingling of the spine
Foreshadowed the appearance
Of my only valentine.

I had no thought of courtship
At that far-distant date;
One girl was like another,
So why, then, concentrate?
One pearl was like another
To this self-centered swine
Who was surfeited with sameness
And knew no valentine.

Just five and thirty years ago
I danced with mind astray,
And suddenly the sameness
Was forever swept away.
I hardly heard the music
I couldn't taste the wine,
For, lovely as a legend,
I saw my valentine.

Oh, lovely as a legend,
Or a silver birch in spring,
And haunting as the twilight song
That hidden thrushes sing!
How I elbowed through my fellows
As they stood in penguin line!
How I dodged among the dancers
As I sought my valentine!

The orchestra played waltzes,
Blank faces swirled about;
I have no foot for waltzes,
So we sat the waltzes out.
Came the tunes of Kern and Gershwin,
But I liked the terrace fine;
Till the band played "Good Night Ladies,"
I wooed my valentine.

Just five and thirty years ago
I walked the earth alone,
The shortest five and thirty years
That earth has ever known.
Young love is well remembered,
But why long for old lang syne
When tonight she is beside me,
My beloved valentine,
My fairest valentine,
My dearest valentine,
Through five and thirty precious years
My own true valentine.